S K I L
JUDO

Brian Caffary
4th Dan

in association with

Des Marwood 1st Dan

A & C Black · London

First published 1992 by
A & C Black (Publishers) Ltd
35 Bedford Row, London WC1R 4JH

© 1992 Brian Caffary and Des Marwood

ISBN 0 7136 3604 1

A CIP catalogue record for this book
is available from the British Library.

Typeset by Latimer Trend & Co. Ltd, Plymouth
Printed and bound in Great Britain by
Whitstable Litho Printers Ltd, Whitstable, Kent

Right Tori (on left) counters uke's attempt
at osoto-gari by throwing him with
osoto-gaeshi (*see page 34*)
Below Sensei Caffary (on the left) watched
by students as he demonstrates the art of
breaking balance, in this case withdrawing
his left hip, pulling with the left arm and
breaking his opponent's balance to the right
front corner

Acknowledgements

Gratitude is expressed to Ealing Borough Council and Twyford Church of England School for the use of the dojo at Twyford Sports Hall, and to their manager, Mr Tony Roberts, for his help in arranging facilities for photographs to be taken there.

Thanks also to Sensei Caffary's students who so generously devoted their time to modelling the techniques featured in this book, and to Sylvio Dokov for taking the photographs.

Sensei Caffary (4th dan) stands on the left of the picture alongside co-author Des Marwood (1st dan) behind dan grade students who performed the techniques photographed for use in this book. They are (from left to right) Robert Brent, Alex Caffary and Peter Brent

CONTENTS

I dedicate this book to the memories of Sensei Kenshiro Abbe (8th Dan) and Sensei Masutaro Otani (7th Dan) who gave me so much education and encouragement in the world of judo.

Brian Caffary (4th Dan)

INTRODUCTION

Over many years judo has been the subject of countless publications printed throughout the world in many languages. Some of them have been anecdotal or historical textbooks, recounting the emergence of judo from its martial art roots into a combat sport enjoying global popularity and Olympic recognition.

Many books have been illustrated instructional manuals for beginners and a relative few have provided specialist knowledge for more advanced students.

Skilful Judo has quite a rare position amongst these extremes, providing as it does a reference work for the student who is beginning to advance; the beginner who has got through the initial trials and tribulations of becoming a judoka or 'Judo man' (or woman), and is now poised to set off in pursuit of serious knowledge concerning both the physical and spiritual potential of judo – The Gentle Way.

Judo attracts students from both sexes, and from all ages and walks of life. Everyone abandons his social, professional and business status within the outside community to lose it in the levelling anonymity of a plain white judogi. He subjects himself to the discipline of a dojo and to the commands of his sensei, to whom he shows great respect.

Some set out upon their judo careers by taking a formal beginners' course at a leisure centre or evening institute. Others attend what are now regarded as old-style clubs in which beginners are pushed in at the deep end to engage in endless randori. These beginners must learn as they go, relying for instruction upon whatever a higher grade may have time to gasp out to them in between sessions of combat. There is little instruction in anything so basic as ukemi, and the beginner eventually comes off the mat nursing unnecessary bumps and bruises.

With today's more serious attention to safety standards, many beginners thankfully start judo by joining a recognized club affiliated to one of the major national organizing bodies. Such clubs have licensed instructors and a properly structured syllabus taking the student through various waza in relation to a kyu syllabus.

Sadly, however diverse the routes by which a student comes into judo may be, so too are the reasons for the early departure of so many of them from the sport. For, like any other leisure-time pursuit, judo has its natural rate of drop-outs long before students have had a full and proper taste of the fruits.

Some disappear almost as quickly as they arrive. Many drift away as early as 5th kyu (yellow belt). Others may leave around 4th kyu (orange belt), for it is then that the physical going can begin to get tough and the mental work on theory become more intensive. In some organizations, it is also the beginning of the study and execution of kata, as it becomes an imminent part of syllabus qualification.

It is perhaps understandable then that this is very often the stage at which deserters decide that judo's not for them after all, and they vanish in search of the nearest squash court, football pitch, gymnasium or just an armchair.

Some of them are a sad loss to judo, but perhaps more important is the manner in which judo is a sad loss to them. In most cases, they are on the brink of beginning to discover the essence of judo and to appreciate and understand what the sport is all about. They will have already swotted up on a bit of basic history and theory, memorized a handful of Japanese words, gone through the occasional pain barrier and endured the sometimes painful monotony of countless breakfalls in practice.

In fact, they will have made a considerable personal investment upon which their quitting will result in a no-return yield. The same, incidentally, reflects upon their sensei, but that is by the way.

Those who do remain in judo beyond this relatively early turning point soon discover, however, that they've barely scratched the surface of judo skill or knowledge. What has been acquired is a minute part of what may be learned. At the same time, the beginner student may be encouraged in the knowledge that what has been learned, however small, is the base, or part of the base, upon which the future is built. Like building blocks, techniques become placed one upon the other to form links in knowledge or to form counter-attacks or combination movements, or to provide the root for some more advanced concept altogether.

The learning process is one of learning and consolidation, followed by more periods of learning and consolidation. This process may be endless, particularly when it takes the student into areas that are not directly concerned with competitive body contact.

There are any number of administrative support roles, all of which require study and the gaining of formal qualifications – timekeeping, scoring, refereeing, judging, first aid, coaching awards and the gaining of higher dan grades. All of these areas, and the degree of certificated knowledge that they demand, are part of the unfolding plains stretching outwards in front of any judoka, and provide reasons for so many being able to enjoy an involvement with the sport into the years after contest days are over.

It is during these years of study, at a point that is never constant among individuals and can never be forecast, that a judoka's outlook on life may become aligned with the general philosophy of judo. This is gradually reflected in attitudes adopted to others out of the dojo in everyday life, as well as towards partners or opponents in randori and contest situations. In this way, judo contributes to all-round character development to the benefit of the individual and society in general.

It is hoped that *Skilful Judo* will stimulate the advancing beginner into reaching out for some of these endless pastures of knowledge and skills and thereby maximize for himself the full benefits of what may be achieved. At the same time, his dedication will provide judo with the type of judoka upon which the future of the sport depends.

Skilful Judo devotes most of its illustrative space to the demonstration of techniques that, whilst outside the range of most syllabus work and therefore not part of any grading examination, can prove to be invaluable in a contest situation.

Similarly, there are counter and combination demonstrations for both nage and katame-waza. None of these is difficult or complicated, and most kyu grades should find them useful to practise and apply in either randori or actual contest work.

Read, discuss, practise and consolidate!

Note Throughout the book individuals are referred to as 'he'. This should, of course, be taken to mean 'he or she' where appropriate.

JUDO'S HERITAGE

The study and practice of judo provides the opportunity to develop mind and body into a state of combined efficiency. This helps to create within the individual a spiritual and physical harmony from which life in general may become more enjoyable and fulfilling, to the benefit also of others around that person. Similar philosophies are associated with all martial art disciplines with roots planted firmly in the ancient East.

Much is spoken about this 'mystique', but little is ever documented and put on record. Perhaps it is because, rather than being something that can be taught and learned by imitative Westerners, it is more an attitude arrived at through experience. It cannot be set down in the same way as a strict syllabus of techniques. It is more a spiritual awareness that comes upon different judoka in different ways and at different stages of their judo careers. To some, especially those who abandon judo at too early a stage, it may never come at all.

Jigoro Kano

Professor Jigoro Kano, founder-father of modern kodokan judo, wrote in a 1930s booklet about judo, published by Japan's then Board of Tourist Industry: 'Judo is a study and training in mind and body, as well as in the regulation of one's life and affairs.'

From his study as a very young man of different methods of attack and defence, Professor Kano became convinced that all depended upon the application of a single principle. This principle was: 'Whatever the object, it can best be attained by the highest or maximum efficient use of mind and body to that purpose.' Kano claimed that, once understood, this principle may be applied beneficially to all aspects of life, whether inside or away from, the precincts of dojo life.

'This principle of maximum efficiency,' he wrote, 'when applied to the perfecting of social life – just as when applied to the co-ordination of mind and body in the science of attack and defence – demands first of all, order and harmony among its members and this can only be attained through mutual aid and concession, leading to mutual welfare and benefit.'

Relating this principle of maximum efficiency to judo in a physical sense, Professor Kano preached and practised the skilful art of the defender harnessing his own power, or energy, to that of an opponent. It is achieved, in simple terms, by the defender multiplying his own power by pulling when the attacker pushes, and pushing when the attacker pulls. Reacting in this manner, at just the right split second of an encounter, the defender is able to turn defence into attack. Kano was able to demonstrate how a relatively small person could use the principle to exploit to his own advantage the superior strength of a larger opponent.

'What does this "gentleness" of "giving way" really mean?,' asked Professor Kano, and continued: 'To answer this question, let us suppose that we estimate the strength of man in units of one. Let us say that the strength of a man standing in front of me is represented by ten units, whereas my strength, being less than his, is represented by seven units.

'Now, if he pushes me with all his force, I shall certainly be pushed back or thrown down, even if I use all my strength against his. This would happen because I used all my strength *against* him, opposing strength with strength.

9

'But if instead of opposing him I were to give way to his strength by withdrawing my body just as much as he had pushed, taking care at the same time to keep my balance, then he would naturally lean forward and lose his balance. In this new position, he may have become so weak (not in actual physical strength but because of his awkward position) as to have his strength represented for the moment by only three units . . meanwhile, by keeping my balance, I retain my full strength as represented by seven units. Here, then, I am momentarily in a superior position and can defeat my opponent by using only half my strength, that is half of my seven units, or three-and-one-half against his three.

'Now', concluded Professor Kano, 'if I had greater strength than my opponent, I could of course push him back. But even if I wished to push him back and had the power to do so, it would still be better for me first to give way because by so doing I should have greatly economised my energy and exhausted my opponent's.'

Kenshiro Abbe

Similar attitudes and benefits are derived from the gentle kyu-shin-do philosophy of the British Judo Council, as set down by their late founder-President Kenshiro Abbe (8th Dan).

Of the three components of the composite kyu-shin-do, kyu means to study, or seek. Shin is difficult to translate and is referred to as 'cosmic nuclear struggle'. Do, as we know from the word judo, means the philosophical, or moral way.

The three precepts of kyu-shin-do are:

banbutsu-ruten: all things existent in the universe are in a constant state of flux
ritsu-do: the motion is rhythmic and flowing
chowa: all things work and flow in harmony and accord.

The philosophy itself propounds that, since creation, the universe has been controlled and governed by the principle that all things transmigrate. The Laws of the Universe are: (i) The Law of Transmigration, (ii) The Law of Rhythm, and (iii) The Law of Harmony.

'Kyu-shin-do,' Abbe once explained in a set of papers outlining the doctrine of the British Judo Council, 'is the understanding, through knowledge and experience, of the principles of the universe and the understanding of the true way of life through Japanese judo.

'We can enjoy the highest form of life by mutual understanding between oneself and the universe and by harmonizing with all things in general . . . the universe revolves and therefore always keeps perfect balance and must have a centre and radius governed by geometric motion . . . every student of judo shall strive to perfect and harmonize by relaxing first his mind and then his body . . . this idea conforms to nature.'

Abbe then stated what must be the spiritual gratitude of the human being to the principle of universal harmony: 'this gratitude is the first and foremost love, and the first step to communication with all people. This leads to love towards parents, friends and all things in the universe . . .

'. . . all life of any kind in the universe has a continuous flow of circulation and transmigration. For instance, we consume food and expel the waste. The donor is ready to give and he who does not ask or think of getting a return will surely be compensated by someone else. Similarly, if a man robs someone else, he in turn will be treated likewise.

'The practice of judo is the same in principle.'

In a physical sense, British Judo Council players attempt to carry these principles onto the mat, with great attention to smooth movements through techniques performed in circular patterns by flowing bodies under the control of relaxed minds.

Respect for one another

However, whether the parent philosophy is kodokan or kyu-shin-do, the end product of intelligent study should be a person of combined and well-balanced mental and physical capacity. The qualities are displayed on the mat by the manner in which players show respect and politeness to each other.

Even in serious combat at contest level, the victor will appreciate the vanquished for the opportunity provided to execute his superior skills. The vanquished will acknowledge, may even admire, the superiority of the victor. Victor and vanquished will exchange and retain respect, one unto the other.

Each has contributed his maximum effort to what is called judo. Each has given of his best, and the outcome has been accepted with humility.

In more simplistic Western terminology, you get out of life only what you put into it – 'as you sow, so shall you reap'. If judo only encourages life to be lived to those principles, then a worthwhile contribution must have been made to the development of harmony among people.

If the philosophy of any Eastern martial art discipline appears shrouded in 'mystique', its physical roots and origins are often more so. However, this is not the case with the roots of modern kodokan judo, the school whose judo is practised by other schools and clubs throughout the world and that is recognized as the sport's governing body by the International Judo Federation and the organizers of the Olympic Games.

Kodokan judo

The kodokan judo discipline came about in fairly recent times, having been created by the late Professor Jigoro Kano, who was born in Himeji, west Japan, in 1860. Kano was well educated, having studied literature, politics and political economy to graduate from Tokyo Imperial University in 1881.

During his academic studies, the young Kano found time to research and study jujitsu (or jujutsu, as it's sometimes called). He was puzzled that, despite the differing principles between one school and another (and there were very many in existence), none seemed to grasp what he called the true essence of jujitsu, the underlying principle applicable to all techniques, which he believed could be achieved by applying maximized total efficiency of both mental and physical energy.

He set about transforming the art of jujitsu from the martial art form that its name indicated into judo, a 'way' or a form concerned more with the all-round development of a person.

It's interesting to note that one old Japanese martial art school, the jikishin-ryu, had been using the name judo in connection with their particular style of combat for some 200 years before Kano appeared on the scene. It was to save any confusion with jikishin-ryu judo that Kano eventually gave his discipline the name of kodokan judo.

Professor Kano made a close study of three of Japan's many jujitsu schools – kito-ryu jujitsu, tenjin-shinyo-ryu jujitsu and yoshin-ryu jujitsu. From each he deleted any techniques that he considered too dangerous, or maybe fatal, to conform with what he was to call kodokan judo. Some jujitsu techniques he adapted; others were of his own creation. Together they composed a martial art form that was possible to practise in safety as a competitive sport. It is often forgotten, though, that many jujitsu techniques are still to be found in some of the more advanced judo kata. These deep techniques could be very dangerous and any kata that features them is taught only to dan grades.

Professor Kano's kodokan school of judo was officially opened in 1882, when he was only 23 years of age. 'Ko' means 'teaching'; 'do' means 'the way'; and 'kan' means the hall, or 'place of learning'. So, the name inferred that Kano instructed the 'way' of life by his own judo.

Kodokan judo prospered, and so did that taught and practised by the Butokukwai, a school set up in 1895 for the study of all Japanese samurai disciplines such as kendo, aikido, kyudo as well as other physical pursuits. In fact, the Butokukwai was at one time the only national governing body of judo in Japan, boasting a multi-million membership. However, Butokukwai's activities were 'curtailed' by the American forces sent into Japan after the end of the Second World War. The more refined and sport-orientated Kodokan School of Judo continued and, thanks to the tireless globe-trotting work of Professor Kano, eventually became recognized by the International Olympic Committee (IOC) as the world governing body of judo.

Sadly, Kano died on board ship in 1938 when returning to Japan from an IOC meeting (at which he was his country's representative) in Cairo. He never lived to see his own sport become an Olympic event. Neither did he see its common language, philosophy and practice spread across the world.

PREPARATION AND TRAINING

A dojo training session is primarily for training and the teaching of judo skills. It is not a general gymnasium for fitness training; any warming up or loosening up exercises performed before or after instruction must not be mistakenly thought of as a keep-fit routine.

Preparing the body for a judo session or cooling it down afterwards are all part of judo.

Otherwise, how much time a judo instructor devotes to exercise routines depends very much upon the length and frequency of the training sessions. It is fair to say, though, that in general the average student is expected by sensei to present himself in a reasonably fit condition and to spend some time elsewhere doing whatever is thought necessary to maintain physical standards.

Just what those standards should be, or need to be, varies among students, and depends very much upon the extent of their judo aspirations. An unfit student from the lower kyu grades will find it difficult to exploit whatever limited skills he possesses with any ease or proficiency. On the other hand, a very fit and agile kyu grade with little skill may provide an energetic challenge to almost anyone during randori.

An unfit but skilful dan grade may find no difficulty in coping with the attacks of a fit kyu grade, or even some fellow dan grades. However, unless outstandingly skilful, the same unfit dan grade will find it impossible to live on the mat with another who is in a fit condition.

So, all other things being more or less equal, a fit player at any level must always have some advantage over an unfit peer.

These, then, are the two distinct parts to any judo training programme – judo skill training and judo fitness training. Many judo players participate in other sports, and this helps them to maintain some acceptable standard of fitness. But one sport does not equip anyone naturally with the right sort of fitness for another sport – far from it: athletes who are fit and competent in other sports have found judo to be exhausting to their physical and respiratory resources.

Having established a reasonable standard of fitness in order to play a sport such as squash or rugby, the average low-key judo club player can probably manage without any real supplementary fitness training programme. However, some supplementary programme may be necessary for the judoka preparing for a contest in a forthcoming grading examination; it would certainly be advisable for any judoka preparing for a serious contest and absolutely essential for the judoka who is determined to make a mark as a regular competitor at area or national level.

A judoka who goes that far with contest work will, if successful, probably be invited to join squad training sessions. These are usually organized and run by instructors who have been, and maybe still are, 'contest' people of high calibre. They, probably more than a club sensei, will have the time to pay greater attention to fitness.

Even then, an instructor can do no more than point the way. It's up to individual judoka just how hard he works at maximizing his physical fitness potential. Physical fitness is a very personal possession. It cannot be given to a person, it cannot be bought; it must be worked for – and often hard. As with other aspects of judo, it demands dedication and commitment.

For many years it was considered that judo randori was the best fitness-building exercise. Nowadays, physical training for specific sports has mushroomed into a whole science in itself. This has caused coaches and instructors of 'the old school' to re-examine what were often the practices of a lifetime, very often to the benefit of sport, it must be said.

However, by whatever route the subject is approached, a fitness training programme for participation in one of the world's toughest body contact sports must be designed to help any judoka acquire the balance, agility, muscle power, speed and stamina required to achieve success and fulfilment.

Additionally, the judo player's make-up should be such that, while remaining calm and cool of mind, his body is able to react at flashpoint into an outburst of explosive action.

A good background support to any fitness training programme may be provided by regular alternative sports such as squash and rugby football. Running is also excellent, providing it is varied, with alternate bursts of jogging, striding out and sprinting, running backwards and sideways straddle jumping.

Exercises

Specific exercise routines can be worked out for individuals at a local gymnasium or leisure centre. They are usually staffed by qualified instructors who are able and willing to give

Three students hurl themselves forwards to perform mae ukemi (forward breakfall)

They land with faces turned sideways to avoid possible injury, toes turned under to raise the knees and body clear of mat, with impact being absorbed by flat hands and forearms

advice on circuit training, specialist development exercises, etc.

Alternatively, there are many exercise routines conducive to good judo fitness that may be worked through without any expensive equipment. These can be performed at home or in a corner of the dojo during a quiet period. Perhaps, with sensei's help, it may be possible to evolve a programme of exercises that is most suitable for an individual's requirements, but one that at the same time helps with the development of all-round body strength through neck, arms, hands, upper body, back, stomach, legs and even ankles and feet.

Legs

Legs contain the body's most powerful muscle groups, and their importance in judo cannot be over emphasized, particularly in groundwork where their use is so often overlooked or ignored.

One of the simplest, yet most effective, exercises for the strengthening of leg muscles is a series of old-fashioned knee-bends, but don't go down from a standing posture into a crouch position. Instead, stand upright with legs together before sinking slowly, with back straight and upright, to a position just above a half-knee bend. At this point, the loading on your knees and thigh muscles will seem to have reached a maximum. Hold the position for a few seconds before rising again to an upright stance. Repeat this movement slowly and rhythmically for as many times as you are able, gradually increasing the number of movements at each session.

If you're already sufficiently well developed in that area, try the same exercise, but standing on one leg only, with the other outstretched to the front. Repeat on alternate legs.

Up-and-down jumping squats astride a bench, side-to-side jumps over a bench, and squat thrusts, are all good exercise routines for those important legs.

Arms

For the arms there's the ever-popular press-up routine, but rather than setting out to break speed records, concentrate on slow, long rhythmic movements with controlled breathing. Speed up to quick ones with handclaps

A
With a passive partner, the student practises uchikomi, an exercise to speed up entry into techniques. He faces his partner (A), then turns in (B) (*see p. 15*) and then right out again (C) (*see p. 16*), repeating this in–out movement an agreed number of times before following through to complete a throw on the final turn-in

between, by all means. Single-arm press-ups, especially when lying sideways, can also be included for more variation.

While considering press-ups, it's as well not to forget pull-ups. Pull-ups, to some sort of bar around which the hand has to grasp, are good exercise for fingers and thumbs, which must acquire a strong grip. It's surprising just how comparatively weak a grip is possessed by even a regular weight-training body-builder who has built up massive arm muscles largely by pushing against bars, but rarely being required to grip.

A good grip is important to a judo player, and to this end much attention should be paid to often-neglected wrists, fingers and thumbs. Strength may be built into them by flexing, the rolling and squeezing of a small rubber ball, or finger-tip press-ups.

B

One gripping exercise, which also benefits the wrists, requires a simple piece of equipment created from a length of strong string or thin rope, which is tied around a brick or some weighty object. The loose end of the rope is attached to a pole or broom handle. With arms outstretched, parallel and at full length, let the hands hang down to take a grip of the pole either side of the rope fixing. Grip the pole and, with slow deliberate movements, curl the wrists upwards, alternating with a downward snatch to catch the pole before the weight can drop to the ground. When the weight becomes rolled up to the top, reverse the curling action on the wrists and lower the weight. Repeat this exercise a number of times, increasing the number on each occasion.

c
Uchikomi practice

Flat on his back, the student raises his left leg

He swings it over beyond the right leg, rolling the whole body in the same direction

He continues rolling to the right until the body is supported tripod-fashion between his forehead and two feet, with the toes turned under. Then he rolls slowly over onto his back again, repeating this several times in each direction to both the left and right sides. Apart from the exercise value of this movement, it is one well worth developing as an aid to escaping from beneath an opponent in groundwork

Back and abdominal muscles

There are numerous well-known exercises for building back and abdominal muscles, but one single, space-saving and comparatively low-budget piece of equipment for use in this area is a good medicine ball.

It is important to note that all that has been explained or recommended in connection with judo fitness training programmes is applicable to adults only. The approach to fitness training for junior players (i.e. those under the age of 16) is naturally less severe. In any exercise routine, great attention is now given to the protection of growing physiques that have not yet reached maturity. Excessive or undue strain placed upon young skeletal structures can easily be the root cause of problems in later life. Immature tendons, joints and muscles must all be protected during their formative years.

Too little attention has been paid to this in the past, and the ogre of a parent (for instance) who is pushing and pushing his offspring beyond his natural abilities in any sport, is no longer a figure of fun. In fact, anyone contemplating the teaching of any sport to any child, should first of all (if resident within the United Kingdom) make contact with the National Coaching Foundation for guidance and advice.

One aspect of training and preparation for judo fitness that is too wide a subject in which to become involved in any detail, is that of diet – your food intake, your nutrition. It is safe to

say that the average judo player, even competitor, eats nothing more than an ordinary well-balanced diet. Progress into the contest area with really serious intent and you'll find that, like a sports car, your engine will then need specal fuels to get the best from it. Then is the time to seek professional advice.

The left leg is raised to demonstrate the thrust position . . .

. . . and is then pushed vigorously outwards. The student takes care to push strongly, rather than actually kicking, which is, of course, illegal in judo. This routine is practised a number of times with alternate legs, again perhaps as an aid to escape from beneath by fixing the foot of the raised leg against an opponent's hip or groin, and attempting to roll him over sideways

The student takes up a defensive position on his back with both knees raised

NAGE-WAZA

Kuzushi, tsukuri and kake

Prior to any attack, tori begins with kuzushi. This is the art of pulling and pushing an opponent around the mat and exploring his stability until there's a point at which he's rocked off balance and is vulnerable.

It may be that he's off balance to the rear, to the right or left rear corner, left or right side, straight forward, or to the left or right front corner.

Whichever is the case, tori must take an instant, split-second advantage of his opponent's direction of weakness to attack with an appropriate technique and move into tsukuri. This is the art of combining your body, arm and leg movements into the correct position for whichever attacking technique has been decided upon. A well set up tsukuri, or 'form', will help to ensure that the technique is performed properly and most effectively.

Finally comes kake, which is the completion or execution of the technique.

This almost anatomical break-down of a throwing technique may seem slow, but all three components are blended together into a single flash of action.

Early kyu grades are generally quite adept at learning the names of throwing techniques, even in the Japanese language. They go through the physical motions of the techniques and probably perform them with varying degrees of proficiency at grading examinations.

Thereafter, the tendency is for the execution of any technique to become faster and faster – not because it is necessarily becoming more skilful, but because it's just getting sloppier. This is too often apparent during randori, but any good instructor will soon spot these bad habits.

The student adopts a strong standing posture . . .

. . . and then drops into a strong jigotai, or defensive posture

20

They not only cease to create effective judo, but they can present dangers to others on the mat.

One remedy is a procedure that all may benefit from if it is gone through fairly regularly at any stage of our judo careers. It is to practise all techniques, with a cooperative partner, at something like half speed so that every unit of movement may be controlled and corrected if necessary in order to achieve maximum effect.

In this controlled manner, the student will come to understand through experience the making of kuzushi, tsukuri and kake, and will eventually speed up to incorporate them skilfully into randori and shiai attacks.

Listed below are forty techniques contained within the basic gokyu, or syllabus, of kodokan judo. The reader should be familiar with most, if not all of them, so for each one I have provided a coaching comment or word of guidance.

Te-waza (hand techniques)

Tai-otoshi (body drop)

Bend low and turn your head in the direction of the throw. Don't drag your opponent in to your own body; use your hand and arms to tip him over your trailing leg.

Ippon-seoi-nage (one-arm shoulder throw)

This can be an effective technique for use against a taller opponent, especially if tori turns in low with the knees bent in readiness to raise his opponent clear of the mat.

Morote-seoi-nage (two-arm shoulder throw)

As with ippon-seoi-nage, morote relies for success principally upon tori's ability to turn in low on an advancing opponent and exploit his forward momentum to help to carry him through and into the throw.

Morote-seoi-otoshi (shoulder drop)

The basis of this technique is the harnessing of the arm movements of morote-seoi-nage with the leg action of tai-otoshi, but, in contests, some choose to sink on to the knee of their trailing leg.

Tori has turned in fully on uke and is about to snap his right leg straight and pull through with his arms to complete tai-otoshi (body drop), one of the classic te-waza (hand techniques)

Kata-guruma (shoulder wheel)

If you place your feet too far apart as you step in deeply to execute this spectacular technique, you may have difficulty in raising your opponent clear of the mat.

Sumi-otoshi (corner drop)

As with uki-otoshi, sumi requires plenty of patience and practice to perfect a technique in which there is no body contact, but only reliance on timing and strong arm action.

Uki-otoshi (floating drop)

This is a throw that epitomizes the very essence of judo by the manner in which tori exploits the advancing opponent's energy by converting it into a force for use against him.

Koshi-waza (hip techniques)

Uki-goshi (floating hip throw)

Remember that tori's hip turns in only so far as (say) uke's belt knot before almost flicking him off and pulling him round with close body contact to complete a classic throw.

Harai-goshi (sweeping loin throw)

Don't develop a chopping action, practising rather the co-ordination of a twist of the hips with a long, smooth backward leg sweep on either the left or right side.

Tsuri-komi-goshi (resisting hip throw)

More so even than with the other hip throws, the lower down your turn-in, the greater will be your leverage and the more effective the end result of your tsuri-komi-goshi.

Hane-goshi (spring hip throw)

This is one technique for which you may find it preferable to slide your right-hand grip on your opponent's lapel up to the back side-collar in order to pull him close in as you turn.

O-goshi (major hip throw)

Practise freeing your right arm from an opponent's left-hand grip in order to have it free to encircle him or even grip the back of his belt, in order to pull his body in close.

Ushiro-goshi (rear hip throw)

Care must be taken when completing this technique to step back so that when your opponent lands, he will be clear of your own feet.

Utsuri-goshi (changing hip throw)

Timing and strength are important ingredients in the execution of this counter technique. It's also essential that the exponent's hips are thrust well forwards to maximize lift.

Koshi-guruma (hip wheel throw)

In uki-goshi, the attacker's hip is driven half-way round into his opponent's abdomen; in o-goshi, both hips are driven in squarely; but in koshi-guruma, both hips pass right through, and uke is thrown across the side of tori's back.

Tsuri-goshi (lifting hip throw)

There are two forms: ko-tsuri-goshi, in which the encircling arm goes beneath uke's armpit to grasp as in o-goshi, and o-tsuri-goshi, when the encircling arm grasps the back of the opposite shoulder or the belt.

Sukui-nage (scooping throw)

This throw is ideally suited for use by strongly built players as a counter attack launched exactly at the moment when an opponent is turning out of a failed attack.

Ashi-waza (foot and leg techniques)

Hiza-guruma (knee wheel)

This is ideal for use against an opponent who comes walking towards you with straight legs – a bad habit that you should never acquire. Always stand or walk with your knees relaxed, or slightly bent.

O-uchi-gari (major inner reaping)

As your pointed-toe foot sweeps away your opponent's leg, don't forget the use of your arms, particularly the one holding his lapel, which pushes against his chest and helps to thrust him backwards.

Osoto-gari (major outer reaping)

Similarly, while your strongly sweeping leg appears to be doing all the work, don't forget the effective use of your arms to break your opponent's balance to the back corner.

Sasae-tsurikomi-ashi (propping drawing ankle)

As with other foot and leg techniques, practise both right- and left-sided attacks, which can be made without changing your normal grip on the sleeve and lapel.

Ashi-guruma (leg wheel)

The pointed-toe sweep of your attacking leg, combining with the co-ordinated twist of your upper body, leaning backwards in line, and the twist of your arms, is an action that you can rehearse solo.

Harai-tsurikomi-ashi (sweeping drawing ankle)

The speed and subtlety required for success with this may best be achieved, as with many techniques, by practising it slowly, step by step, with a partner.

Deashi-barai (advancing foot sweep)

This is another technique that you can practise solo, perfecting the art of retaining balance on your back foot while performing the pull–push arm action and making a powerful leg sweep.

Kouchi-gari (small inner reap)

Even the accomplished sometimes find it difficult to retain their own balance when executing this technique, so always be prepared to follow through into groundwork as your opponent falls backwards.

Kosoto-gari (minor outer reaping)

This is a crisp technique that, when properly applied, can bring about swift results with apparently little effort – especially useful as a counter throw at close quarters.

Kosoto-gake (small outer hook)

The word gake indicates that this technique is applied with a hooking leg action, rather than the extended leg sweep of kosoto-gari, of which at one time it was regarded only as a variation.

Uchi-mata (inner thigh reaping)

Apart from the fact that uchi-mata is useful for combination with other techniques, the technique is in itself such a potential winner that it has become very popular in contest judo.

Osoto-guruma (large outer wheel)

This technique is very similar to osoto-gari, except that tori moves in much deeper to take both of his opponent's legs; it is also useful as a counter against an opponent's osoto-gari.

O-guruma (major wheel)

Some mistake it for harai-goshi, others think it's ashi-guruma, but properly executed there's no mistaking o-guruma, as the sweeping leg across the front of an opponent makes contact with his upper front thigh, or even lower abdomen.

Okuri-ashi-barai (side sweeping ankle)

Dependence upon speed and timing makes this another technique for use against stronger, heavier opponents who have feet scooped sideways from beneath them, rather than being drawn forwards as with deashi-barai.

Ma-sutemi-waza (rear sacrifice techniques)

Tomoe-nage (stomach throw)

This is a very spectacular throw, which can be achieved only by stepping deep between your opponent's legs, drawing his upper body close into your own to provide low pivot, and extending your right or left leg fully to propel him over your head as you fall backwards.

Tori has stepped in deep between uke's legs as he drops backwards onto the mat, shortening his arms to break uke's balance forward while placing the sole of his right foot against uke's left hip in readiness to throw him over his head in one fluent and spectacular movement (tomoe-nage)

Ura-nage (rear throw)

This is one of few occasions when you'll be breakfalling backwards from a standing position, so keep your own head bent well forward to avoid whiplash onto the mat.

23

Sumi-gaeshi (corner throw)

Co-ordinate the combined actions of your drop backwards to the rear corner with the pull of your hooked foot around your opponent's inner thigh to get maximum power into this throw.

Yoko-sutemi-waza (side sacrifice techniques)

Yoko-gake (side dash)

This throw is sometimes called 'side body drop' or 'side hook' (as the name gake implies). The exponent should keep the pulling arm well into his own body to maximize the pull as well as to protect the elbow as he falls sideways.

Yoko-otoshi (side drop)

Feint quickly before changing the direction of your main attack, and your opponent's own momentum will help to topple him over your outstretched leg.

Tani-otoshi (valley drop)

This throw is similar in execution to yoko-otoshi, but in this case your opponent is thrown onto his side, rather than onto a back-corner shoulder.

Yoko-wakare (side separation)

This is too often regarded only as a sacrifice throw, and the opportunity is therefore missed to employ yoko-wakare as a superb counter technique by stepping round an opponent's hips and countering attacks such as seoi-nage, uki-goshi, o-goshi, etc.

Uki-waza (floating throw)

Not usually a syllabus subject, uki-waza has remained one of the sport's finest techniques throughout judo history, having been practised by many masters.

Hane-maki-komi (outer winding spring hip)

This is one of several throws in which the basic overarm action of soto-maki-komi is combined with the leg action of another technique – in this case, hane-goshi.

Yoke-guruma (side wheel)

Yoko-guruma is another sacrifice technique that can serve you well as a counter against any attack that offers you a leading leg around which you are able to step.

Shimmeisho-no-waza

Since the original formulation of the gokyo-no-waza and the revisions that the Kodokan made to its list of officially recognized throwing techniques in 1920, 17 more have been accepted.

These, referred to as shimmeisho-no-waza, include some that are not permitted for use in randori or shiai and have therefore been omitted from the range demonstrated on the following pages. Some others are counter techniques and therefore overlap with the content of the following chapter, which is devoted to kaeshi-waza.

Morote-gari (two-handed reap)

Morote-gari (two-handed reap): tori steps in deeply between uke's legs, driving his shoulder firmly against the opponent's body with arms encircling both legs just above knee height

Both of uke's legs are scooped upwards

Tori retains a controlling hold of uke's legs as he is thrown backwards onto the mat

A

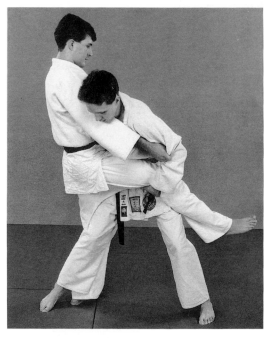

B

Kuchiki-taoshi (one-handed drop) photos 20–22

A Kuchiki-taoshi (one-handed drop): tori releases his grip on uke's right sleeve as he steps in deep between the opponent's legs

B Driving against uke's upper body, tori grasps his opponent's leg behind the right knee and scoops upwards

C Continuing with the upward scoop of the leg, tori pushes his right hand and forearm against uke's body to throw him backwards onto the mat

C

Kibisu-gaeshi (heel trip)

A Kibisu-gaeshi (heel trip): tori steps forwards to place his left foot along the outside of uke's right foot, simultaneously bending to grasp from the inside around the back of uke's ankle with his right hand

B Pulling uke's right sleeve downwards with his left hand, he sweeps the right leg higher with his right hand

C This downward and upward pulling action takes uke off balance, and he falls onto his back

A

B

C

A

B

C

Uchi-mata-sukashi
(inner thigh reaping slip)

A Uchi-mata-sukashi (inner thigh reaping step-around): uke (on the left) turns in to attack with uchi-mata

B As uke completes the turn and swings his attacking right leg, tori moves his left foot away to a position behind his right foot

C Tori keeps tight hold of uke, adjusting his balance to both feet and using his opponent's own momentum to carry him forwards into a handthrow onto the mat

A

B

Kani-basami (scissors throw)

A Kani-basami (scissors throw): tori has stepped across to place his right foot to the outside of uke's right, and now pivots on that right foot while sweeping his left leg backwards across the front of uke at stomach height

B Simultaneously, tori places his right hand on the mat for support as he swings his right leg across the back of uke's knees to apply a leg-sweeping scissors action

C Tori's vigorous pull on uke's right sleeve helps to propel him backwards as both legs collapse and, as they land, tori is in a good position from which to move into groundwork if necessary

C

A

B

C

Osoti-maki-komi
(outside wrap-around throw)

A Osoto-maki-komi (major outer wrap-around throw): tori releases his right-hand grip from uke's left lapel to swing it over uke's right arm, as he pivots towards his own left and begins a sweep with his right leg

B Uke begins to roll forwards as his right arm becomes firmly curled around tori's turning body, with tori's right arm still swinging round to clamp it further

C As he must with all maki-komi techniques, tori fully commits himself to the attack, sweeping with his right leg and continuing to spiral to his own left so that he is in the position of advantage as they land on the mat

A

B

c Uchi-mata-maki-komi (inner thigh wrap-around throw)

A Uchi-mata-maki-komi (inner thigh wrap-around throw): in another maki-komi technique, tori releases his right-hand grip of uke's left lapel and swings it strongly over his opponent's right arm, while turning in for a normal uchi-mata

B With uke's right arm firmly trapped around his spiralling body, tori completes his leg sweep as he spins to his left

C Uke has been spun round completely and tori lands beside him, still grasping that right arm

31

A

B

C

Harai-maki-komi (sweeping loin wrap-around throw)

A Harai-maki-komi (sweeping loin wrap-around throw): as tori turns in to sweep with harai-goshi, he releases his right-hand grip of uke's lapel to swing it over his opponent's right arm

B Tori pulls uke's body around him; the right arm is trapped against him as he continues spinning to his left

C Tori's spinning sweep brings them both down onto the mat, with uke on his back

A

B

Tsubami-gaeshi
(swallow counter)

A Tsubami-gaeshi (swallow counter): uke attempts to attack with a deashi-barai, but is foiled by tori, who is able to raise his right leg clear of that sweeping left foot

B Tori circles his right foot over uke's left foot to strike it on the outside and continue momentum with a counter sweep

C Tori's sweeping right foot has carried through to achieve a counter that takes uke off his feet

C

A

B

C

Osoto-gaeshi
(outer reaping counter)

A Osoto-gaeshi (major outer reaping counter): uke (on the right) has moved in to attack with osoto-gari

B Before he can be caught properly off balance, tori rocks forwards and starts a counter reap with his right leg

C Tori drops his right leg to regain balance as uke is countered and thrown

O-uchi-gaeshi (major inner reaping counter)

O-uchi-gaeshi (major inner reaping counter): tori (on the left) is able to resist uke's attempt to attack with a right-handed o-uchi-gari (*see over page*)

Tori instantly sweeps uke's right leg away, across his own front

Pushing strongly off his back foot and using his arms effectively, tori sweeps right through so that uke lands on his back

A

B

Kouchi-gaeshi (minor inner reaping counter)

A Kouchi-gaeshi (minor inner reaping counter): uke (on the left) swings his right foot forwards to attempt kouchi-gari against tori's right leg

B Tori has time to withdraw his right leg out of range and, as uke's swing continues, tori assists the momentum with a steering-wheel arm action to take his opponent off balance to the rear right corner

C The counter has been completed, and tori is in full control and ready for any further action

C

A

B

C

Hane-goshi-gaeshi (spring hip counter)

A Hane-goshi-gaeshi (spring-hip counter): as uke turns in to attack with hane-goshi, tori sinks his hips to resist and prepares to sweep his opponent's supporting left leg with his own left foot

B Using his arms effectively in support of his left leg counter, tori sweeps uke into the air

C Uke lands at tori's feet and, if ippon is not awarded, tori is well positioned to go into groundwork

A

B

Harai-goshi-gaeshi (sweeping loin counter)

A Harai-goshi-gaeshi (sweeping loin counter): uke (nearest the camera) swings up his right leg to attack with harai-goshi

B As tori drops his hips to resist attack, he curls his left leg against uke's supporting left leg

C Tori has swept uke's left leg across to their right and has quickly regained his own balance before uke lands on the mat

C

A

B

Uchi-mata-gaeshi
(inner thigh reap counter)

A Uke has turned in to attack with uchi-mata

B Tori resists by dropping his hips and, as uke withdraws the attacking leg, tori prepares to sweep away his opponent's supporting leg with his left foot

C Tori's left foot sweeps away uke's supporting left leg and, combined with positive arm action, tori sends uke on his way to the mat

C

KAESHI-WAZA

As an opponent moves in to attack, you are often able to defend by blocking his technique in some way or other. Then, his attack being foiled, the pair of you remain tense and locked together for an energy-sapping instant before the attacker moves out.

The contest carries on to consist of little more than single attacking techniques – blocking, turning out and turning in – especially if the defender has no knowledge of kaeshi-waza. Such procedure is not only very tiring, with no real advantage to either contestant, but it is frankly poor judo!

On the other hand, a defender with a knowledge of kaeshi-waza (counter-attacking techniques) will be able to keep the action flowing to his own advantage, as well as to conserve energy.

The principle of a successful kaeshi-waza, or counter-attack, is based upon the defender taking advantage of an attacker's weak moment to launch his own attack. The counter-attack needs to be a technique that moves along the same line of force as that of the original attack. To do this, the defender withdraws whatever part of the body is necessary from the direct line

Tori has thrown uke with uke-waza (floating throw) to counter his opponent's attempt at tai-o-toshi (body drop)

41

of the attacking movement, and executes his own technique. This technique may be any that will propel the original attacker along his own line of energy force, as he is pulled (hopefully!) off balance and into a throwing technique of some sort.

There are two instances when an attacker is most vulnerable to kaeshi-waza. The first is the split second he begins to turn in on an opponent. The second is when, having completed the turn in but failed to complete the technique, he begins to turn out again. In both

Tori has countered uke's deashi-barai attack with tsubami-gaeshi, reaching the peak of his left foot counter sweep (see page 33). Tori follows through with a positive arm action to assist in breaking uke's balance and throwing him to the mat (see right)

instances, the full force of his body is pulling, pushing or being propelled by his own energy in a certain direction. It is that energy force that the defender must harness to his own use if a successful counter technique is to be applied with good effect.

As with renzoku-waza, there are too many countering movements to list, and in any case they are reactive and impulsive. You can only *feel* when an opponent is vulnerable to them. Begin by practising, with a partner, the examples shown on the following pages. Think about the principle, and more will come to you naturally through experience.

A

B   C

Harai-goshi (sweeping loin throw) countered with Ushiro-goshi (rear hip throw)

A Harai-goshi (sweeping loin throw) countered with Ushiro-goshi (rear hip throw): uke has turned in fully to attack with harai-goshi, but tori is able to resist being moved

B As uke's attack falters, tori thrusts his hips forwards and upwards, assisting lift by a firm grip on uke's jacket lapel with his right hand, while his left hand grasps the back of his opponent's belt or jacket

C As tori straightens up fully, he flicks his hip to throw uke off him and onto the mat, retaining hold of him as he does so in order to have control over any ensuing groundwork

A

B

Hane-goshi (spring hip throw) countered with Ura-nage (rear throw)

A Hane-goshi (spring hip throw) countered with ura-nage (rear throw): uke has turned to attack with hane-goshi, but doesn't prove strong or quick enough to move tori instantly

B Tori immediately grasps the initiative by stepping his right leg forwards and round, and placing his right hand flat in the centre of uke's stomach so that he's almost facing his opponent

C Pulling with his left hand on the back of uke's belt or jacket and pushing with his right, tori spins himself around and backwards in ma-sutemi-waza (rear sacrifice technique) to complete his ura-nage with uke falling over his left shoulder

C

A

B

C

Uchi-mata
(inner thigh reaping)
countered with
Sukui-nage
(scooping throw)

A Uchi-mata (inner thigh reaping) countered with sukui-nage (scooping throw): as uke has turned in to attack with uchi-mata, tori has stepped around the attacking leg

B Pictured from the other side, tori can be seen simultaneously grabbing the inside upper thigh of uke's trouser leg

C Gripping the trouser leg in one hand and uke's lapel in the other, tori lifts uke in the air against his body, which leans backwards before he flicks his opponent clear and steps back to remove his feet from the landing area and to complete a reverse variation of sukui-nage

Uke has attacked with an attempt at osoto-gari but has been firmly resisted by tori (on right), who prepares to turn his hips to the left and counter with osoto-gaeshi as demonstrated fully on page 34

RENZOKU-WAZA

Renzoku-waza (combination techniques) are similar to kaeshi-waza in as much as, when applied, they keep a contest active and flowing with sustained effort, rather than it becoming a stop-go-stop-go composition of a series of single-technique attacks and withdrawals.

The big difference between the two groups of techniques is that renzoku-waza are performed by the attacker. Having had a first attacking technique blocked by the defender in some way, the attacker will not withdraw, but will take any advantage that he can of the position in which he finds himself, by transforming the basis of the original foiled attack into the application of a quite different attacking technique. Naturally, the attacker will need to re-think and move quickly at lightning speed into his alternative attacking combination before the defender can apply any kaeshi-waza.

Whatever renzoku-waza the attacker may use as his follow-through technique, he will make use in energy terms of either his own established line of propulsion or of the energy expounded by the defender in attempting to block, turn or pull away from the original attack.

As with kaeshi-waza, the list of possible follow-through or combination techniques is innumerable. They are performed spontaneously and instinctively. Their common denominator is that their line of execution follows lines of established energy forces.

Moving from standing into groundwork is a simple combination of two different groups of techniques, whilst grappling itself is very often a series of one technique following upon another until an effective result is achieved.

A succession of techniques that may be linked for practice purposes (almost as an

Uke has stepped over that outstretched leg to foil tori's attempted tai-otoshi, but tori can continue attacking by pivoting even further to his left and sweeping the right leg upwards and attacking with uchi-mata. Alternatively, if uke decides to pull away backwards, tori may move in the same direction and use his right leg to curl around uke's left leg and take him backwards with ouchi-gari or gake

informal kata) is shown in the following pages. There's nothing hard and fast about them. Intersperse them with your own ideas if you think that something suits you better. Overall, practise such moves diligently, primarily familiarizing yourself with the art of movement from one technique to another. Begin to appreciate maximum force for minimum energy. Let things flow . . . that's good judo!

And a final word, which also goes for kaeshi-waza: practise your combinations on both left and right sides of attack.

Tori attempts o-uchi-gari . . .

. . . fails and switches attack to kouchi-gari . . .

. . . withdraws his right leg and attempts to reap with osoto-gari . . .

. . . then pivots on his left foot for tai-otoshi

Tori sustains the attack by curling in his right leg for hane-goshi . . .

. . . and then sweeps it up for harai-goshi before . . .

. . . sweeping his right leg between uke's legs and attempting uchi-mata

Tori drops his right foot to the mat, turns completely in on uke and attempts ippon-seoi-nage

From the ippon-seoi-nage attempt . . .

... tori outstretches his right leg and moves for seoi-toshi ...

... making a full turn ...

... and throwing uke to the mat

As tori drops into the kami-shiho-gatame variation, he passes his right arm around uke's arm to grasp uke's jacket high on the right shoulder . . .

. . . while his left arm curls beneath uke's armpit to grip the rear shoulder of uke's jacket, thereby trapping the right arm as he drops onto his opponent

He maintains his control of both trapped arms as he moves round . . . .

. . . until he's in a variation of yoko-shiho-gatame with uke's left arm even more securely pinned

Tori counters uke's left-footed sweep with tsubami-gaeshi . . .

. . . and pushes it through until it's pinned against uke's own right leg . . .

. . . as he pivots into ippon-seoi-nage . . .

. . . and throws his opponent

Again, uke attempts to sweep and tori allows the impetus to help him pivot on his left foot and turn in

He bends well forwards as he swings his right foot away from uke's sweeping foot . . .

. . . before sweeping his own right leg up and alongside the outside of uke's thigh . . .

. . . to throw him with an effective harai-goshi

OSAE-KOMI-WAZA

When reviewing the whole range of katame-waza (grappling techniques), it is usual to begin with osae-komi-waza (hold-down or pinning techniques). Generally it is how good or bad you are with osae-komi-waza that will determine the success or failure of your attempts at related locks or strangles, whether they be executed by you or against you, when on the ground.

Become able to control an opponent on the ground with some confidence, and you'll then be in a position to apply related skills. Allow yourself to be dominated in osae-komi-waza, and you'll be the one who is vulnerable to arm-locks, strangles and hold-down 'ippon' defeats.

It is important not to overlook the needs of groundwork in any supplementary fitness training programme that you may undertake. Belly-crawling and shuffling at speed back and forth, face downward as well as on the back, should be part of your routine. Bridging – and

Tori demonstrates groundwork follow-through when, after throwing uke with tomoe-nage . . .

... he retains a two-handed grip on his opponent and uses the momentum of the technique to roll himself over his opponent's head ...

any other programme designed to strengthen both back and stomach muscles – is beneficial.

And don't forget those legs! It's amazing just how many quite experienced kyu grades go into groundwork apparently forgetting that they still have legs, just because at the time they're not using them to stand up on. If used correctly, legs and feet are a source of powerful support when you are grappling on the ground. In attack, they provide a base from which to push and exert control. In defence, they serve almost as an extra pair of hands and arms, encircling, pushing and even gripping.

On the ground, there are points of balance to be disturbed and exploited exactly as in nage-waza (throwing techniques), with an opponent's supporting knees or arms (instead of legs or feet) being swept away to bring about imbalance or even a collapse flat onto the mat.

Conversely, never lose sight of the need to take your opponent's legs 'out of it', as they say. Control them whenever possible by trapping or taking a grip on one or both in such

a way that they are raised from mat contact to become neutralized and ineffective.

If you are the attacker, maintain maximum body contact with your opponent at all times during osae-komi-waza. If you are the defender, then work to create gaps between your body and that of your attacker: gaps through which arms or legs might be pushed to provide the beginning of a counter move.

The average student spends too little time with what might be termed 'useful training' in groundwork. Working in pairs, the roles of tori and uke should be alternated. While uke remains supine and offering only token resistance, tori starts with (for example) yoko-shiho-gatame and then moves around uke, over and back again, working positively yet smoothly through the whole range of standard and variation techniques.

Too much time and energy is so often spent practising groundwork in a manner that consists of nothing beyond one of the partners, having dominated the other, settling down into a

. . . and into a perfect tate-shiho-gatame hold-down position

secure hold from which few would have any chance of escaping. As a training exercise, this does no one any good at all. The superior performer, having proven his ability, should loosen his hold and move to apply alternative techniques. Then, if one partner is significantly superior in attack, they should change roles completely so that the dominant partner practises defence from underneath, while his partner attacks from on top.

This is perhaps the point, though, at which to underline and remind students that it is not necessarily the player who is underneath who is the defender. Some groundwork specialists prefer to attack from underneath, drawing an opponent close down upon them in order to apply some form of favourite strangle, or arm-lock.

A careful study of the techniques depicted on the following pages will hopefully give you some fresh thoughts about the application of osae-komi techniques.

Kesa-gatame (scarf-hold)

Kesa-gatame has become one of the most popular hold-downs, maybe not so much because it's among the first of any groundwork techniques taught to beginners, but because it can be so neatly dropped into from a wide range of other techniques.

When expertly applied, with the attacker leaning his full bodyweight properly onto uke's rib-cage, kesa-gatame can be quite painful and result in a submission well before any count has been completed for a hold-down.

When applying the hold-down, maintain a strong tripod base support from your resting hip and two feet. Don't freeze into a set position. Be prepared to counter uke's attempts at escape. Keep shuffling on your bottom to retain full body contact, and re-position your legs constantly to foil any attempt that uke might make to hook his legs around your trailing leg and break the hold with tok-e-ta.

With his head tucked in low, his legs spreadeagled and uke's right arm trapped firmly in against his body, tori applies the standard kesa-gatame. His right arm encircles uke's neck and, with thumb inside, he grasps the back of the collar. It is a tight, secure hold

Leaning slightly back and applying weight against uke's rib-cage, tori removes his right hand from around uke's neck, slips it beneath uke's left armpit and places his forearm on the mat with a flat hand (palm downwards). This completes kuzure-kesa-gatame (broken scarf hold)

Tori applies another variation of the scarf hold, known popularly as the 'pillow-hold'. Tori brings his right knee higher until his thigh reaches behind uke's head. Tori removes his grip from behind uke's collar and rests it palm down on his own thigh, as near as possible to the back of uke's head. Tori leans his body-weight into uke's right shoulder

Ushiro-kesa-gatame (reverse scarf-hold)

Although it is possible to transpose the position of your legs from the basic hon-kesa-gatame and shuffle round into this ushiro-kesa-gatame, or reverse scarf-hold, the position of tori is so radically different as to qualify it almost as a completely separate technique.

Also, rather than being a hold-down into which you might drop naturally from a standing posture, it is almost always a technique that you might well find yourself rolling into in the course of some general groundwork grapple.

As with the basic kesa-gatame, keep the head tucked well in to foil any attempt at a strangling counter. Lean well back onto uke's *upper* rib cage in this instance, but do not cover his face so that breathing is obstructed.

Tori has dropped into ushiro-kesa-gatame, with uke's right arm pulled tightly across the front of his body. Tori's left forearm rests on the mat, with his elbow tucked in somewhere near to uke's armpit and his left hand grasping the left side of uke's belt

Tori has now varied his grip, slipping his left hand beneath uke's left arm, which becomes trapped as tori grips the left side of uke's jacket

Having thrown his opponent with a maki-komi technique, tori retains hold of uke's encircling right arm, places his own right forearm and hand flat on the mat for support, and drives off his spreadeagled legs into uke's rib-cage. Tori must keep his head well forwards, with his neck protected from attack by uke's left arm

Tate-shiho-gatame (trunk holding)

Tate-shiho-gatame is a hold-down that you can roll into immediately as a follow-through to tomoe-nage, providing of course that you've maintained a grip on your opponent's jacket from which to pull yourself into a backward roll, ending up in a straddling kneel across his chest.

There are several variations of the manner in which your arms may encircle and trap your opponent's head and arms. Whichever you use, don't bend so far forwards that you become unbalanced so that your opponent is able to bridge and roll you off over his head. Another safeguard against this happening is to pin your own legs limpet fashion, and with feet tucked well in, around your opponent's body.

Tori applies tate-shiho-gatame, encircling uke strongly with his arms while squeezing with his knees and keeping his feet pointed downwards. His toes are well tucked in against his opponent's lower body

As uke struggles and raises his arms in an attempt to apply some escaping technique, tori gathers them both together above uke's head

Uke is more helpless than ever with his arms finally trapped in what for him is a weakening posture, and tori leans fully forwards with his head tucked in low to press home his advantage

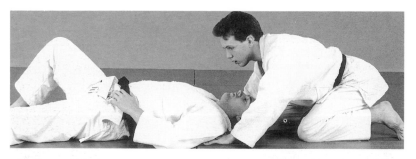

Tori, in kneeling posture above uke's head, prepares to slide his hands with a flat palm down beneath uke's shoulders

Tori has slipped his hands forwards to grasp each side of uke's belt, squeezing uke's arms inwards to limit their use in any counter-attack. His kami-shiho-gatame complete, he will bear down on uke and additionally control his opponent's attempts at rolling into an escape with the constant repositioning of his legs

Seen from the other side, tori is moving into kuzure-kami-shiho-gatame (broken upper four-quarter hold). Tori has released his right-hand grip on uke's belt and curled his right arm around uke's arm, which becomes trapped as he passes his right hand through uke's armpit to grasp his opponent's jacket at a point behind the right shoulder

Kami-shiho-gatame
(upper four-quarter hold)

Rather than being a straight follow-through from a standing technique, kami-shiho-gatame is generally employed in the course of grappling for advantage during groundwork.

Maintaining full body contact with uke, who is face upward on his back, tori may be swivelling around on top in search of a grip. Then, when kami-shiho-gatame, or any variation of it, is applied, tori flattens his body down onto uke. His legs are extended, with toes turned in, as he drives his weight down onto his opponent.

Again, the use of legs is important. Uke's legs are out of tori's control, making it all the more important that tori uses his own legs correctly to counter what will be strong and vigorous attempts by uke to bridge and roll his way out of trouble.

Tori moves in to apply yoko-shiho-gatame by first taking hold of uke's belt with his left hand and then threading his right hand between his opponent's legs to grip the back or side of the belt

Tori encircles uke's neck and grips deep around the back of the collar, with the thumb inside. He drops down into yoko-shiho-gatame

As uke struggles in an attempt to escape, tori has released his grip on uke's collar and has brought his left arm forwards and around uke's left arm to take a grip behind uke's jacket. Tori completes this kuzure-yoko-shiho-gatame (broken side four quarter) by forcing his forehead to the mat and preventing uke from rolling to his left. Attempts at rolling to the right are controlled by tori's use of legs

Yoko-shiho-gatame (side four-quarter hold)

Once tori has applied yoko-shiho-gatame, it's important to turn his head to face that of his opponent. This simple move helps to negate any attempt that uke might make to apply a strangle by drawing a lapel across his throat.

As with most hold-down techniques, tori controls uke's attempts to roll out of the hold-down this way or that by crouching or extending his own legs in counter movements thereby retaining control of uke's body.

Should this fail to stop uke from rolling outwards and away from the hold-down, tori can apply further prevention by placing the top of his head down on the mat, close into the far side of uke's body. At all times, tori must maintain full body contact.

Tori demonstrates a basic kata-gatame, with hips raised as he drives strongly off the rear foot to bring his full weight close in to secure uke's body

Tori has moved slightly forwards and around uke's trapped elbow in order to apply more pressure with his left arm and head, while his right hand has gone over the top of uke's shoulder to secure a grip with his thumb on the inside of uke's collar and drawing uke's wrist tightly against the side of his neck

In this variation, tori has scooped uke's left arm into the hold. He has also pushed it over the top of uke's trapped right arm and has grasped the wrist with his left hand. Tori's scooping right arm has passed around the outside of uke's upper arm to grip the back of uke's collar, securing a painful technique and bringing nearer the submission that can come from a good kata-gatame

Kata-gatame (shoulder hold)

When applying kata-gatame from (for example) your opponent's right side, ensure that his body movement is minimized by wedging your bent right knee as firmly as possible against the side of his rib-cage. This will prevent him from attempting an escape by rolling inwards, towards you.

Pressure on his right shoulder, as your weight is driven down upon it from your extended left foot and through your raised hips, should lock him in and prevent any attempt to roll away from you.

Kata-gatame is a hold-down that you can sometimes drop into from a standing posture, following a throw, in preference to kesa-gatame. During groundwork in either randori or shiai, you may well find yourself able to move into kata-gatame from a kesa-gatame that is proving not to be too secure.

SHIME-WAZA

No grade is ever too high to be given the basic reminder of the need for safety when either practising strangles or applying them in randori or shiai. If uke taps in submission, tori's release must be instant and immediate. Conversely, uke must be aware that dead heroes are not appreciated on the mat, and nothing is to be gained by hanging on endlessly without submission, once a strangle has been firmly fixed. Sooner (rather than later!) you're going to become asphyxiated and pass out.

Many players forget, or overlook, that shime-waza is comprised not only of pure strangles, but also of chokes and some techniques that are a combination of both. Generally, though, they are all referred to as

Sensei Caffary demonstrates an alternative method to that shown on page 73 of using the head to apply additional pressure during hadake-jime. Here, Sensei Caffary's head is pressed hard against the side, not the rear, of uke's head. This increases pressure against uke's carotid arteries in the side of his neck, as opposed to only affecting the thorax at the front 'strangles'. However, a *strangle* is effected when pressure is applied to the carotid arteries located below the ear on each side of the neck. A *choke* is the result of restrictive pressure against the windpipe. Some techniques apply simultaneous pressure to the windpipe and cartoid artery, as well as to the jugular vein.

When applying shime-waza from the front (kata, nami and gyaku-juki-jime, etc.) it cannot be emphasized too much that to become effective, the attacker should slide deeply into either side of an opponent's collar before locking on the grip. The technique becomes effective as soon as the gripping fists are screwed in or outwards, as the case may be, so that the bony parts of the knuckles (or wrist) press against the arteries in the side of the neck.

Properly applied, such strangles should have an immediate effect. If they don't, then it's likely to be because you've committed the novice error of not going in deeply enough to grasp your opponent's collar. Don't waste time and energy trying to squeeze a result from a technique that is basically flawed. If it can't be

corrected, move into another technique.

Careful training and practice will determine just how long you can hold out against an attacking shime-waza. Experienced players develop the knack of some resistance by raising shoulders to shorten their neck and expand their neck muscles. The full effect of some strangles may be at least delayed by turning your head *towards* the direction from which the strangulating force is coming, and not *away* from it as most would do by simple instinct.

The arm, or both arms, of the attacker may be vulnerable to some defensive counter moves. If the attack is from behind, across your throat, draw in your chin, try to push the offending arm upwards, and attempt to slide your body downwards.

It is possible that none of these recommendations will provide fully effective resistance or escapes. At worst, you may still have to tap in submission. At best, you might just have delayed sufficiently until 'Time!' is called for the end of a contest, while the points decision is still in your favour.

Tsuki-komi-jime (thrusting choke)

Although tsuki-komi-jime can be applied while standing, tori is seen here applying the thrusting choke from a kneeling posture. As he thrusts, tori turns his right fist with the back uppermost and draws the left lapel of uke's jacket across his throat to the right. The technique tightens as tori pulls downwards on uke's right lapel with his left hand

Uke is able to survive the attack long enough to grasp tori's forearm with his own right arm, push with his left hand on the back of tori's elbow and pull downwards to escape and counter with ude-gatame (arm crush, or straight arm-lock)

B

Tomoe-jime (circular strangle)

A From the rear, tori reaches with his left hand around uke's neck and grasps uke's left lapel. Simultaneously, tori crosses his right arm over his left to grip the left side of uke's back collar, with the thumb on the inside. Tori twists his wrists and bends his arms as he leans forwards to apply an effective strangle from which a submission will doubtless follow

B Should uke be able to resist the full effects of the attack and not tap in submission, tori may apply extra force by pressing his own head in against that of uke

A

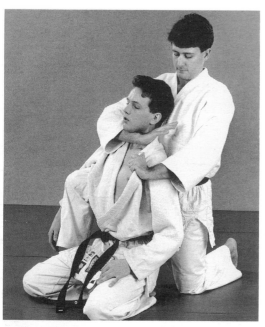

Okuri-eri-jime (sliding collar strangle)

To make sure that he gets the deep entry necessary to make this okuri-eri-jime most effective, tori opens up uke's left lapel so that he can slide the thumb of his right hand as far as possible up the left front side of uke's collar, before taking a grip and clamping his forearm across uke's throat

Tori's left hand has now slipped beneath uke's left armpit to pull downwards on the jacket lapel. He leans slightly backwards if necessary to give the technique added strength

Kata-ha-jime (single wing strangle)

Tori demonstrates kata-ha-jime, going in deep around uke's throat with his right hand. He traps his left arm (wing) in the air with his left as that hand travels through uke's armpit, upwards to the front and round to the back of uke's head. Tori's left hand is clenched as he forces uke's head forwards with the back of his fist

In this case, before the strangle becomes fully effective, uke has countered and escaped by reaching his right hand up to grasp tori's jacket at the right shoulder, thrusting his right foot backwards and rolling tori over his own right shoulder as he lunges forwards to his front right corner

Hadake-jime (naked choke)

From the rear, tori has drawn the bone of his forearm tightly in across the front of uke's throat. Then, from underneath, he clasps his left hand with his right, using down leverage against uke's shoulder to force the right arm upwards and to make the strangle effective

Again, an attack across the throat from the rear becomes more effective if tori lowers his head to push against that of uke

Kata-juji-jime (half cross strangle)

Tori kneels astride uke to apply kata-juji-jime. The fingers of one hand take a deep inside grip on the opposite collar of uke's jacket, with the thumb outside. The other arm crosses over the top to the collar opposite, but with the thumb inside and fingers clenched on the outside. Tori shortens his arms and leans forwards to increase pressure and achieve submission

In this instance, tori's kata-juji-jime is not effective quickly enough, and uke has time to counter. Uke threads his right arm over tori's left arm and under his right to join up with his own left hand as he attacks tori's right elbow joint. Pushing on the elbow as he turns his body to his own right relieves the pressure of tori's strangle, and he could eventually roll further into attack

Nama-juji-jime (normal cross strangle)

Tori has come up between uke's legs, but as he applies nami-juji-jime, uke grabs his right forearm with his right hand and pushes on that elbow with his left hand. Simultaneously, uke swivels his hips from beneath tori and pushes downwards with his right leg to collapse tori's left knee support

Uke continues swivelling to his right side. Using both hands to trap tori's right arm in a lock against the elbow, uke completes his counter-attack by swinging his left leg up over tori's shoulder and leaning backwards as he levers it against the side of tori's head in order to gain a submission from this hold, which is called ashi-gatame

Gyaku-juji-jime (reverse cross strangle)

Tori has moved in between uke's legs to apply gyaku-juji-jime – fingers in deep on each side of the collar, with both thumbs on the outside – but uke is quick enough to grab both of tori's sleeve elbows, pulling them outwards and upwards to add leverage when he pushes his feet against tori's knees so that their support will be removed and tori will collapse forwards

As tori is flattened, uke draws up both of his knees in a reflex action, and clamps them firmly against the outer sides of tori's elbow joints, squeezing them inwards and probably getting a submission

KANSETSU-WAZA

As with shime-waza, there's no disgrace in tapping to submit the moment you feel that an opponent has secured you positively and firmly in an effective arm-lock. Conversely, release your opponent the instant he taps if the positions are reversed.

Probably the best advice to give anyone about arm-locks is never to be caught by such a technique. Although that is easier said than done, most opponents often give some indication of what they are grappling for before they actually achieve the full lock. Think quickly,

In facing kneeling postures, tori extends his right leg so that his foot pushes uke's supporting knee away to the rear. This disturbs uke's balance, enabling tori to take uke with him as he drops sideways to the mat on his right, preparatory to moving into hiza-gatame, the arm-lock shown on page 85

and you may be able to foil such an attempt.

Once you are aware that an attacker is working towards an attack on an arm, do whatever you can to prevent that arm from being outstretched. Grasp it with your own free hand to attempt resistance against the lock, or to pull it free. If possible, move your whole body to a different angle in such a way that it may neutralize your opponent's line of pressure. Curl up, and use your knees or feet to push him away. Maintain your struggle, especially if you are in a contest that is nearing the end, and you are ahead on points.

Of course, there are arm-lock 'specialists' who are so skilful that they are able to lock an elbow without any warning from numerous angles other than those used for standard demonstration purposes.

In practice, the student should rehearse arm-locks and their application in attack from diverse angles as well as to both right and left sides. As with shime-waza, kansetsu-waza can often provide a short, sharp decisive victory in a contest situation.

Always remember that, under whatever circumstances kansetsu-waza is applied, injury should be avoided whenever possible. Joint techniques are injurious unless they are properly controlled. While the defender must recognize superiority with taps of submission, so must the attacker be in full control of his own muscular power when applying strength against the elbow joint.

Waki-gatame (armpit arm-lock)

For waki-gatame to be fully effective, tori must ensure that uke's captured arm has been fully extended and turned over so that tori's armpit drops directly onto the back of uke's elbow joint.

The lock may begin with uke being taken to the ground from a standing posture, or as part of groundwork procedure. Whichever, tori must not allow his armpit to be positioned so high above uke's elbow that it becomes a shoulder lock, which is of course illegal. Also, as waki-gatame, it would be completely ineffective.

As with other arm-locks, the use of waki-gatame is very much an opportunist technique. Practice with a partner will bring about the discovery of the variety of circumstances in which you may have a chance to use this technique.

From either a standing or a kneeling position, tori has pulled through uke's right arm with his own right, spun to his right and looped his left arm over uke's extended arm. As uke has dropped face downwards to the mat under pressure of this attack, it can be seen that the back of his right elbow is trapped beneath tori's left armpit, and this basic waki-gatame in itself is often sufficient to bring about a submission

Failing immediate submission, tori may be encouraged to tighten his grasp of uke's wrist and raise the foream against the elbow joint

To achieve a submission against a very strong opponent, it may be necessary for tori to lean his body well back onto uke to allow space for maximum leverage. He should take care that the armpit's point of contact does not slip up uke's arm so that tori becomes guilty of illegal pressure against the shoulder joint

Juji-gatame (cross arm-lock)

Beginners often remember this technique more easily than some others, not only because it's among the first they ever learn, but also because it is often referred to in English as the 'step-over' arm-lock, and this is descriptive of the first move into the action.

Juji-gatame is usually an immediate follow-through from a throw, providing a good example of the need to retain hold of an opponent's arm as you control his landing on the mat. From this, you are able to move smoothly from nage-waza into katame-waza without a break.

Whatever else you may be doing, juji-gatame will work effectively only if you are skilful enough to position the back of your opponent's elbow joint accurately against the bony side of your groin and apply pressure at that point. Pressure on the joint is increased if you lean well back, pull the wrist of uke's extended arm close into your upper chest, and raise your hips from the ground to force your groin upwards against uke's elbow joint.

Tori has thrown uke and is still grasping uke's right arm. He steps his left leg around his opponent's head and prepares to drop backwards into juji-gatame

Tori drops back into juji-gatame but . . .

... as uke continues to struggle, tori sits up again and grabs the sleeve of uke's left arm, just behind the elbow ...

... so that when he drops back again, tori has both of uke's arms trapped in such a manner that a submission must be secured

Ude-garami (entangled arm-lock)

When asked to demonstrate ude-garami, it's quite amazing how many experienced kyu grades will hesitate and then make one or two faulty attempts, before groping their way into the correct position for the application of this elbow-locking technique. Other players slip into ude-garami quite swiftly and efficiently without any pre-thought during randori or shiai.

Hesitancy results from not practising the lock in slow motion, and studying *how* it's done rather than *why* it's effective. Once the student understands *why*, it becomes automatic to understand *how*. Having grasped the principle of the technique, practice will help you to discover the situations (other than that of the standard demonstration) in which ude-garami may be applied.

Working across uke's upward-facing body to apply ude-garami, the lock may be given added strength if tori leans to press his head down upon uke's elbow joint.

Tori's first move in going for ude-garami on the ground, across an opponent's body, is to use the left hand, palm down, to grip and control uke's left wrist. Simultaneously, tori begins slipping his right hand beneath uke's left upper arm

Tori's right hand has passed beneath uke's left upper arm and has gone through to grip, palm down, over the back of his own left wrist

The ude-garami is now complete, but becomes effective when tori draws uke's left wrist in towards his shoulder, while pushing upwards with his own right forearm. Properly applied, this should bring about a submission from uke

Ude-gatame (arm crush)

In a demonstration, ude-gatame is usually applied by tori kneeling alongside uke, who is lying face upward. As uke reaches with an outstretched arm to grasp tori's lapel, tori clamps both hands around uke's elbow joint and (as the name of the technique suggests) 'crushes' it close against his own body.

Tori may find it useful to raise one knee and wedge it against uke's rib cage to help to control his opponent's body movement.

Although this is the standard position for demonstration purposes, always be on the look-out for an opponent offering you a 'stray' straight arm. This arm crush can be applied from several different postures. Practise a few moves with a cooperative partner.

About to apply ude-gatame on the far arm, across his opponent's prostrate body, tori demonstrates the correct way to gather in the arm by clasping with both hands behind the elbow and positioning the opponent's hand and wrist between the left side of his own face and shoulder (*see over page*)

Tori now turns slightly to his left as he pulls uke's arm close into his body, wedging uke's body close into his knees; the ude-gatame should now be effective

No submission appears to be forthcoming from uke, so tori gets extra leverage by stepping over uke's body with his right foot and, as he leans forwards, the required result will no doubt be achieved

Hiza-gatame (knee arm-lock)

Hiza-gatame is another arm-lock that often results in kyu grades doing this or that before they slip hesitatingly into a demonstration of the technique, which can be begun from either a standing posture or groundwork situation.

Hands, legs, knees, arms and feet are all involved in the application of hiza-gatame, but all it takes to master and perfect is patient practice with a cooperative partner. As with ude-garami, think not only about *how* it's applied, but also *why* it's effective. Once you understand the sense of it all, you'll appreciate the need for the positioning of those hands, legs, knees, arms and feet.

Hiza-gatame, like all other judo techniques, should be practised on both the left and right sides of your opponent.

Tori has taken the initiative in collapsing uke onto his face and, as he leans backwards to pull and straighten out his opponent's right arm, he raises his left knee and prepares to go into the final stages

With his left foot clamped firmly against uke's right hip, tori's left knee has been lowered to assist the clamping of uke's right elbow from behind, and the hiza-gatame is complete

Tori is not satisfied that things seem as secure as they should be, so he swings his left leg upwards, over uke's right shoulder and across the right side of uke's head. Pulling back on uke's arm and pressing down with his left leg against uke's head, tori has now transferred to a hold known as ashi-gatame

CONTEST JUDO

Assuming you have been in judo long enough to be aware of the use of weight categories, scoring methods and rules, attention can now be paid to the deeper psychological aspects of contest judo and how you might prepare yourself to meet with the challenge of taking part.

Randori is practice-fighting against a partner, but when it comes to shiai (contest), the player opposite you becomes an opponent. Any opponent is there to be defeated, though honourably and within the rules of judo. To achieve victory will require all of your skill and fitness. It will also require that essential quality that we call kanka-shein (fighting spirit).

A player may be taught skill and can work to acquire fitness, but 'fighting spirit' is an intangible something that is within each and every one of us to some degree or another. It is the positive side of the 'fight-or-flight' syndrome, the flashpoint that we must control to explode into positive action the instant a referee has brought two opponents to the centre of the mat and called: 'Hajime!'.

It is the stuff of which warriors were made. It remains still the stuff of which judo contestants need to be made. It is there somewhere within each individual, but only he can ignite it from within.

Before defeating an opponent, you must first defeat your inner self in this respect. There is little hope of becoming 'a contest fighter' unless you can first compete with yourself to fire your fighting spirit and create an outburst of energy that, though explosive, can be controlled and sustained throughout whatever period of attack is necessary to defeat an opponent.

There are many ways in which competitors prepare themselves for this. Pre-contest nerves of some extent are common, but they vary from one individual to another. They must be dampened down as the fighting spirit is stoked up to take over. To achieve this, some choose to relax or meditate; while some even fall asleep, or cat-nap. Others may prefer some gentle jogging or exercise, while others exercise vigorously in a state of perspiration. The apparently 'cool' ones are those who appear to carry on normally, chatting with team-mates and watching other contests being fought.

By whatever course you have arrived at it, 'fighting spirit' should have taken you over by the time you are called to the centre of the mat. Dominate your opponent from the outset, but not with the ridiculous eye-balling indulged in by professional boxers on television. Practise, instead, the art of looking deeply without staring, intently without lapsing into a fixed gaze or trance. Don't take your eyes from those of your opponent. Look into them, through them and back again into your mind.

Your mind should show you a miniature television-type picture of what you are about to perform with perfection – a technique that you will move in to execute the moment the referee calls: 'Hajime!'.

You've already summed up your opponent's potential as he walked onto the mat. If you've already seen him performing against other opponents, you may have some idea as to what his first move is going to be, or the style with which he fights.

If he's taller than you, your mental rehearsal will show you swivelling into a low-fulcrum attack such as tai-otoshi, seoi-toshi or ippon-seoi-nage; maybe your own long-leg sweeping power will favour the use of your favourite uchi-mata or harai-goshi.

Hajime: there are no hand signals as the referee calls 'Hajime' for either the start of contest or the resumption after a stoppage

Koka: the referee calls 'Koka' to signify the award of three points, raising his forearm, with the palm facing forwards, to shoulder height

Yuko: the referee calls 'Yuko' to signify the award of five points, and raises a straight arm 45 degrees from the side of the body, with the palm facing down

Wazari: the referee calls 'Wazari' and raises his arm to shoulder height, palm facing down, to signify the award of seven points

Wazari-no-muko: the referee calls 'Wazari-no-muko' and waves his arm back and forth above the head, palm inward, to indicate an invalid technique

Wazari-awaseti-ippon: the referee calls 'Wazari-awaseti-ippon' to signify the award of 10 cumulative points from two wazari scores. He raises his arm, with the palm facing inwards

Ippon: the referee calls 'Ippon' to signify a 10-point score, followed by a 'Sorre-made' call to indicate the end of a contest. The arm is the same as for wazari-awaseti-ippon

Osae-komi: with the palm down, the referee stretches his arm over the players and calls 'Osae-komi' to signify that the timekeeper's recording of hold-down may begin

Osae-komi-to-ke-ta: the referee passes his arm to and fro over the players and calls 'To-ke-ta' to signify that the hold-down is broken and timing may cease

Sono-mama: the referee stretches out his arms, palms downwards, and calls 'Sono-mama' to indicate that players must freeze exactly as they are until he has spoken to them or corrected their position

Yoshi: there are no hand signals, as the referee calls 'Yoshi' for resumption of action after sono-mama stoppage – similar to the call of 'Matte' after normal stoppage

Kogeki-seyo: the referee faces the player in default and rotates his forearms forwards to indicate the need for more action to be displayed

Jikan: the referee calls *'Jikan'* and the arm is outstretched, with his palm facing forwards towards the timekeeper, to signify that the clock is to be stopped for time-out

Hantei: the referee calls *'Hantei'*, with his arm held upwards and palm facing inwards, to indicate the need for a consultation with the judges about a contest end with equal score

Hike-wake: the referee calls *'Hike-wake'* to signify a drawn contest, raising and lowering his forearm to waist level, with the palm facing inwards

Shosha: the palm faces inwards as the referee raises his arm to 45 degrees above the shoulder, towards the winner, calling *'Yu-sei-gachi'* for a win by superiority

Your eyes will still be fixed on those of your opponent. Your breathing will be steady and controlled. Your stance will be relaxed, with your knees not locked straight but slightly bent. There'll be one last flash rehearsal, and at the call 'Hajime!' you'll be pulverized into instant attack.

Perhaps your first planned attack will fail (it often does!), so you'll turn into an alternative combination; you'll block your opponent's counter and attack with one of your own.

Beware the opponent who's slow and ponderous and who looks as though he may enjoy exerting his superiority in groundwork. Take a deliberate decision to go into groundwork with any type of opponent only if you feel reasonably confident of success. Very often it's much easier to hold your own by blocking or countering an opponent's standing attacks than it is to counter or escape from grappling techniques.

Otherwise, sustain your attack, and don't give your opponent the opportunity to settle down and maybe take over the initiative. Your fitness will begin to pay dividends. Counter, block and attack again until the call of 'Ippon!'.

You will (hopefully!) have scored a deserved win. It will have happened so quickly, as everything does in a judo contest. Only through experience will you become aware of the subtleties of contest judo, the tactics and the psychology of it all. There's nothing like contest experience if you want to learn about contest judo. So if you do, get out there and compete!

But whether you are considering a contest career seriously or not, you need to become familiar with the scoring system as well as the hand signals and vocal commands of a referee. All of them, and the signals of corner judges, are the language of contest judo anywhere and at whatever level, be it the Olympic Games, national or area tournament, club competition or grading examination.

In any case, when contest days are over, maybe you'll like the idea of becoming a qualified referee yourself!

KATA

The purist of the Western world would agree with Eastern cousins that within kata is to be found the true essence of judo, while the not-so-dedicated would claim it to be a dull, old-fashioned concept for which there is no place within modern judo.

Incredible though it may seem, others might not even know that kata exists until well into their judo careers, and will never have experienced what kata demands of the students and gives in return. Sooner or later, though, regardless of the particular organization with which players are registered, most do eventually at least become aware of kata. Any member of the British Judo Council, whether male or female, senior or junior, will at 3rd kyu (green belt) level be expected to demonstrate proficiently certain kata, or parts of kata, at grading examinations. Kata is taught at British Judo Council clubs throughout the United Kingdom.

For those who do not know, or are in any doubt, it must be understood that kata is not any one, single mysterious thing. It is best explained broadly as a set of rules for judo contained within a 'form'. Each kata, or 'form', is in the shape of a choreographed sequence of techniques linked together by a common theme and performed by tori with a cooperating uke.

The manner of performance is rhythmic and fluid, and thereby reflects the true spirit of judo. There is a spiritual union between the performers, and plenty of eye contact at strategic stages establishes a silent communication by which their movements are synchronized.

Originally, it was the intention of Professor Jigoro Kano for kata to be the keystone of judo, and his own instructors were examined in their kata proficiency before they were permitted to teach. Kata, with its pre-arranged sequences of techniques performed in a controlled manner, was, in a way, every beginner's syllabus for learning judo. It was through the knowledge of kata that the student became familiar with both the mental and physical aspects of judo.

As has been already explained, there is more than one single kata. Not even a single kata can be fully explained within a single chapter of any book. However, to summarize, there are currently seven forms (or themes) of kata taught at Tokyo's Kodokan, and collectively they are referred to as randori-no-kata.

Nage-no-kata (throwing forms) consists of three from each of the five categories of throwing techniques.

Katame-no-kata (grappling forms) comprises five from each of the three categories of grappling techniques.

Kime-no-kata (forms of decision, or combat) consists of 20 techniques employed in combat situations demonstrating defence and attack considered too dangerous for use in randori.

Kodokan-goshin-jutsu (kodokan self-defence forms) comprises 21 self-defence techniques against armed and unarmed assailants.

Ju-no-kata (the form of gentleness) comprises three sets each of five techniques demonstrating the efficient management of body strength and movement.

Itsutsu-no-kata (the five forms) consists of five techniques of graceful movement symbolizing such forces of nature as the circulation of water and the movement of heavenly bodies.

Koshiki-no-kata (the ancient forms) comprises 21 techniques adapted by Professor Kano from those originally created for use by ancient armour-clad warriors of the kito-ryu (kito school).

Of these various kata, it is nage-no-kata and katame-no-kata that are probably best known to most Westerners, as nearly all of the techniques contained within them are taught as syllabus work by most schools.

Both sets of kata are included in higher kyu grade examinations of the British Judo Council. For similar reasons, ju-no-kata (popularly set down in English as juno-kata) is also well known, knowledge of it being required by female students seeking higher-grade qualification.

Ju-no-kata comprises many techniques that are not taught as standard syllabus work, and so presents any student, male or female, with new challenges. In presentation, the techniques within this kata are more closely linked in physical terms than those included in nage-no-kata and katame-no-kata. The movements are flowing and graceful, with an aerobic quality. At the same time, the movements themselves are a series of self-defence techniques providing the exponent with valuable street knowledge.

Going more into the area of self-defence and unarmed combat techniques, reference can be made to kime-no-kata and kodokan-goshin-jutsu. The self-defence and unarmed combat techniques that they include – kicks, strikes and joint locks – are generally considered to be too dangerous for teaching to lower grades. Nevertheless, they do have the type of content that appeals to many who turn to alternative martial art disciplines such as karate or jujitsu from which, of course, judo was evolved in the first place.

It just so happens that as judo has become more and more a predominantly competitive sport, judo kata has lapsed somewhat and faded into the background. Karate, by contrast, still maintains a strong emphasis upon its kata, but some people fear that, if not carefully monitored, this could wane as karate's appeal as a competitive sport grows.

Judo players who ignore their kata in favour of shiai (contest) can easily become content with practising only the limited number of techniques that they have found adequate to defeat opponents on the road to trophies and medals. They miss out completely on the wider mental and physical aspects of judo that kata has to offer.

Very often, it is the more mature judo player who turns to kata when contest days are over. But that does not mean that the competitive edge has been lost, because there are competitive kata tournaments held at all levels. Competitors are marked for features such as presentation, demonstration and interpretation, for there are wide differences in the various performances of kata by one individual and another.

Kata is much the same as ice skaters performing their 'compulsory figures', equestrians their 'dressage' or gymnasts their 'apparatus work'. Judo kata did have a trial as an Olympic event for women, but was subsequently dropped, which is a great shame because it does leave the true spirit of judo not fully represented at these great international meetings.

Talk to your sensei about kata, which can be as bright and challenging as you want to make it. Alternatively, enquire to the British Judo Council about the availability of their specialist kata instructors and the excellent courses that they run.

From these lists you may familiarize yourself with the make-up of both nage-no-kata and katame-no-kata, but you will require the help of a kata instructor to learn the manner in which they must be performed.

Nage-no-kata (kata of throws)

Te-waza (hand techniques)
Uki-otoshi (floating drop)
Ippon-seoi-nage (one-arm shoulder throw)
Kata-guruma (shoulder wheel)

Koshi-waza (hip techniques)
Uki-goshi (floating hip throw)
Harai-goshi (sweeping loin throw)
Tsuri-komi-goshi (resisting hip throw)

Ashi-waza (foot and leg techniques)
Okuri-ashi-barai (side-sweeping ankle)
Sasae-tsuri-komi-ashi (propping drawing ankle)
Uchi-mata (inner thigh reaping)

Ma-sutemi-waza (rear sacrifice techniques)
Tomoe-nage (stomach throw)
Ura-nage (rear throw)
Sumi-gaeshi (corner throw)

Yoko-sutemi-waza (side sacrifice techniques)
Yoko-gake (side dash)
Yoko-guruma (side wheel)
Uki-waza (floating throw)

Katame-no-kata (kata of the ground)

Osae-komi-waza (hold-down techniques)
Kuzure-kesa-gatame (scarf hold)
Kata-gatame (shoulder hold)
Kami-shiho-gatame (upper four-quarter hold)
Yoko-shiho-gatame (side four-quarter hold)
Kuzure-kami-shiho-gatame (broken upper
four-quarter hold)

Shime-waza (strangle techniques)
Kata-juji-jime (half-cross strangle)
Hadake-jime (naked choke lock)
Okuri-eri-jime (sliding collar lock)
Kata-ha-jime (single wing lock)
Gyaku-juji-jime (reverse cross lock)

Kansetsu-waza (arm-locks)
Ude-garami (entangled arm-lock)
Juji-gatame (cross arm-lock)
Ude-gatame (arm crush)
Hiza-gatame (knee arm-lock)
Ashi-garami (leg arm-lock)

INJURIES AND THEIR TREATMENT

Considering that it is such a hard, body-contact sport, judo is able to boast a relatively low record of serious injury. Much of this applaudable achievement must surely be due to dojo disciplines enforced by instructors and respected by students, as well as to the invaluable duties performed by officials connected with grading examinations and contest judo. At all levels of judo, not only on the mat but also around its precincts, 'safety' is a recognized and respected watchword.

Contest judo, anyway, represents but a small percentage of the total hours spent on mats every day by players training throughout the world. Much more time is devoted to randori and general training, during which the body is subjected to high impact and stresses and strains upon muscles and joints. These sessions can be, and generally are, more than equally arduous to anything experienced in competition, and every attention must be paid to safeguarding participants from injury through either accident or overwork.

In the not-so-long-ago 'good old days', injury was something to which the average judo player paid little attention, unless it was something of an obviously serious nature. The popular treatment for almost anything seemed to be 'Work it off!', and in some miraculous way this is what happened in many instances (apart from cases of concussion or broken bones).

Nowadays, there is a more responsibly minded attitude towards any type of injury following the realization that, unless they are properly diagnosed and treated, some injuries can be the cause of serious physical problems in later life.

A judoka's first thought though, concerning injuries, should be to do everything possible to prevent them occurring in the first place . . . *avoidance* is better than *treatment*! There are many ways in which the injury rate from endeavours on the mat may be at least controlled, from the moment a student steps into the dojo in preparation to go onto the mat.

To begin with, there should be no embarrassment about wearing any elasticated support for suspect or temporarily weakened muscles or joints, whether they be shoulders, elbows, wrists, knees or ankles. Even damaged fingers or toes benefit from being temporarily strapped to their neighbours for extra support.

Particularly during training, many players choose to wear shin guards, though unless there's some particular physical weakness in that area, the shins may well benefit from exposure to toughening-up attacks.

No player should overlook or deliberately bypass the bodily warm-up routine, which is akin to warming up a racing-car engine before driving it out onto the track. The body becomes warm and lubricated, and the adrenalin begins to flow.

Next comes the ritual of ukemi, in which the whole range of breakfalls is performed to both the left and right sides. Beyond that, the student can go into training or actual contest work and probably suffer little more, at worst, than the occupational hazard of bumps, bruises, the occasional mat burn, or an attack of cramp.

The better the quality of judo by both attacker and defender, the less likelihood there is of either sustaining any serious injury. Bodies that are relaxed, in either attack or defence, possess a flexibility that best equips them to react instinctively in accord with any direct force or line of applied energy. A body that is held stiff and rigid is in opposition to the fluid principles of judo, and can be a likely cause of injury to both combatants.

This principle is often illustrated by comparing the gentle, drooping willow tree with the strong, stiff, upstanding oak. The branches of the willow will relax and give way to the weight of (for instance) falling snow, bending until the load slips away of its own accord before springing upright again, undamaged and full of its former strength. On the other hand, the stiff, unyielding branches of the sturdy oak withstand nature's onslaughts to the very maximum, until they snap and break off beneath the weight of attack.

Unfortunately, as in any other sport or walk of everyday life, accidents are not totally avoidable in judo, and they do sometimes happen. The most common types of injuries include loss of consciousness and damage to joints and ligaments of elbows, knees and shoulders, as well as to the back.

Until quite recently, the treatment of many of these injuries was provided on the mat by a senior dan grade experienced in the Japanese art of katsu, if such an official was available. Such officials were able to apply certain forms of resuscitation, relax knotted muscular spasms and re-set dislocated joints. Very often, the injured player would be fit enough to resume combat after treatment.

Probably the only katsu practised on the mat today is kogan-katsu, a method of treating a man whose testicles have been shoved up into his groin and who is in need of immediate release from excruciating pain.

Otherwise, today's judo injuries are treated by mat officials or instructors, who are obliged to have a recognized first-aid qualification from an official organization such as the St John Ambulance Brigade or the Red Cross. Victims of concussion or asphyxiation of any sort are treated in the normal first-aid manner, placed in the recovery position and kept warm while awaiting despatch to hospital for a formal examination and further treatment if necessary.

Any other serious injuries affecting mobility are treated similarly, and after diagnosis the injured is made as comfortable as possible until despatch to hospital takes place.

No manipulation is ever attempted to an injured player on the mat. Such unqualified treatment, as opposed to that of a registered medic, could not only aggravate the injury but also affect any subsequent insurance claim that may be made.

Generally speaking, a St John Ambulance Brigade or Red Cross officer will be in attendance at any properly organized tournament.

At club level, sensei will (or should) have a recognized first-aid certificate, and similar procedures will be followed. Additionally, clubs should be safe rather than sorry by making everyone aware of the nearest hospital with a casualty department, and of its telephone number. One club member who owns a car should be deputed as 'transporter' in the event of an ambulance not being available or not necessary, i.e. if the injured person is a 'walking wounded'.

THE LANGUAGE OF JUDO

The use of Japanese names – and their meanings wherever necessary – throughout this book will have extended any student's Anglo-Japanese vocabulary range. All Japanese is phonetic when written in the English language, but a further break-down of pronunciation in the following list may provide a judoka with help in learning more words from the world of judo.

aiti, eye-ti, partner or opponent
ashi, a-she, foot or leg
ashi-no-ko, a-she-no-koe, instep
ashi-no-ura, a-she-nooro, sole, or ball of foot
ashi-yube, a-she-you-be, toe, or toes
atemi-waza, a-temmi-waza, striking techniques
ayumi-ashi, eye-oomi-a-she, natural walking style

Budo, Boo-doe, spiritual systems for achievement of personal all-round perfection
Bujutsu, Boo-jut-soo, combative fighting systems of Japanese warriors
Bushido, Bush-ee-doe, warrior's way of life – code of honour

chowa, choe-wa, state of mental and physical harmony during practice

daki, da-keye, to scoop up
do, doe, way, or path of life
dojo, doe-joe, training hall, or area

eri, eh-ree, collar or lapel of jacket

fudo-shin, foo-doe-shin, an alert and clear mind
fusegi, foo-seggie, defence
fu-sensho, foo-sen-show, retirement of contestant during tournament, leaving opponent the winner

gaeshi, gay-she, superiority

gokyo-no-waza, goe-keye-o-no-waza, five basic categories of kodokan judo throwing techniques
go-shin (jutsu), goe-shin (jut-soo), body (self) defence

hana, han-ah, nose
hane, ha-nay, spring
hanshi, han-she, highest grade in judo
hara, ha-rah, stomach
harai, ha-reye, sweeping
hidari, hid-arry, left side of player
hiji, hidge-ee, elbow
hiki-komi, hick-i-kommie, pulling opponent to ground without attempting to throw
hiza, hi-za, knee

i-kai-sen, ick-eye-sen, first contest in competition or tournament

jigotai, jig-oh-tie, defensive posture
jogai, joe-guy, outside the mat area
jonai, joe-nigh, inside the mat area
ju, joo, gentle
judogi, joo-doe-gi, judoka's traditional outfit
judoka, joo-doe-kah, judo player

kachikake, catch-ee-cack-ee, chin
kaeshi, k-eye-she, teacher grade
kaiko, k-eye-koh, judo practice
kake, ka-key, execution of a throw
kappo (katsu), cap-oh (cat-soo), resuscitation techniques developed in jujitsu
karu, ca-roo, to reap
keage, key-aggi, kick
koshi, kosh-ee, hip
kube, coo-be, neck
kube-nage, coo-be-naggy, neck throw
kyoshi, k-eye-oshi, teacher grade
kyu, queue, to search mentally, study
kyu-shin, queue-shin, globe, ball or sphere

maki-komi, mackey-kommey, winding technique
migi, midgie, right side of player

obi, owe-bi, belt
omote, omm-otti, front
oshi, osh-ee, pushing

randori, ran-dor-ee, free-fighting practice
rei, ray, bow, or salutation
rei-gi, rei-gee, type, or style of salutation
renshi, ren-she, high-grade teacher
renshu, ren-shoo, free practice, or exercise

shiai-jo, she-joe, contest area
shin-ban, shin-ban, to referee
shin-ban-do, shin-ban-doe, method of refereeing
shin-ban-in, shin-ban-in, referee

shi-sei, shy-say, posture in general
shizen-tai, she-zen-tie, natural posture
sode, so-day, sleeve of jacket

tai, tie, body
tatami, tat-army, mat
tatsute, tatt-suit-aye, referee's command to stand

waki, whacky, armpit
waki-shita, whacky-sheet-ah, under armpit

yoko, yoke-oh, side
yubi, you-bee, finger
yu-sei, you-si, referee's word meaning 'decision'
yusho-sen, you-show-sen, final contest in a
   tournament

INDEX